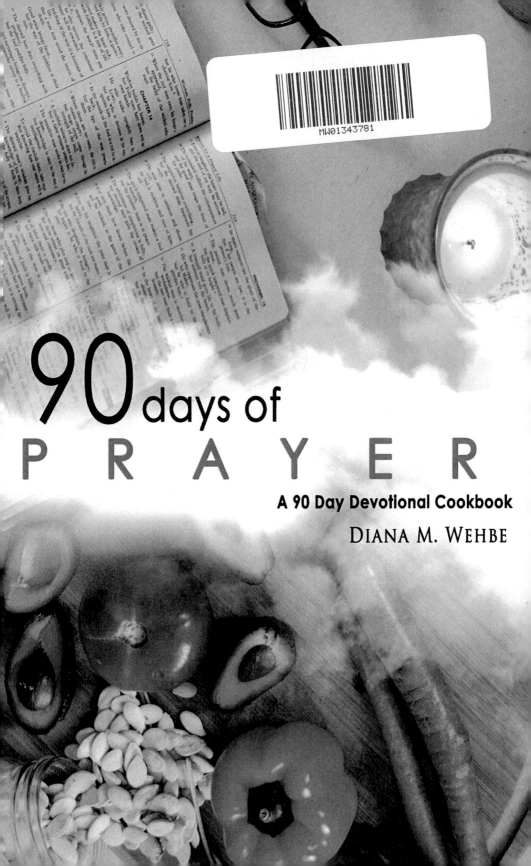

Copyright © 2015 by The Purpose Foundation
ISBN: 978-1519146892

90 days of PRAYER:
A 90 Day Devotional Cookbook

All Rights Reserved. No part of this publication may be reproduced, Stored in a retrieval system, or transmitted, in any form or in any means – By electronic, mechanical, photocopying, recording or otherwise – Without prior written permission.

Scripture taken from the HOLY BIBLE, NEW INTERNATIONAL VERSION®. Copyright © 1973, 1978, 1984, 2011 by Biblica, Inc.® Used by permission. All rights reserved. Scripture taken from the NEW KING JAMES VERSION®. Copyright © 1982 by Thomas Nelson. Used by permission. All rights reserved. Holy Bible, NEW LIVING TRANSLATION copyright © 1996, 2004, 2007, 2013 by Tyndale House Foundation. Used by permission of Tyndale House Publishers Inc., Carol Stream, Illinois 60188. All rights reserved. Scripture taken from the KING JAMES VERSION of the Bible. Scripture taken from the
THE DOUAY-RHEIMS BIBLE.

Edited by: Meilani Darby

Cover design © 2015 | Meilani Darby and David Ambriz
Interior design by Meilani Darby - www.designedbynani.com

This book is not intended as a substitute for the medical advice of physicians. The reader should consult a physician in regards to his/her health and particularly with respect to any symptoms that may require diagnosis or medical attention.

To my Lord and Savior Jesus Christ, my Mentor, my Guide, my Love and my Light, my Eternal Father in Heaven, to You and for You I write, live, work and serve each and everyday of my life. Thank You for saving me, and for the many You will reach in these 90 days.

My hopes for you, the reader: I pray this book guides you to wherever God has been calling you. I have spent too many years of my life walking around lost and confused. I am no longer lost, I am finally found in the arms of my savior, Jesus Christ. I pray these 90 days you take seriously and ask for guidance and motivation to stay focused on the calling over your life. Jesus will never leave you or abandon you. I know this from my experience. May love flow through you unto others and may healing come into your spirit, soul and body. Blessings,

Days 1-30

90 Days of Prayer

DAY 1

When Things Start to Fall Apart...
Let Them.

*"Count it all joy, my brothers, when you meet trials of various kinds, for you know that the testing of your faith produces perseverance." - (**James 1:3**)*

I'm still learning how to let go of things that I should learn to let go of. It's hard! A past relationship, a current relationship that's slipping away or going in different directions, an opportunity that wasn't right for you but you kept chasing it, thinking it could be or was..Why? God has SO much waiting ahead of you.. Just for you! So much to run after that is created for you, that feels right, that doesn't cause you to feel wrong for wanting them. God created you in Purpose and on Purpose...Let what needs to fall apart ...fall, in order for what needs to fall together.

Recipe for the week

Fresh Face Shake

Ingredients:
Spinach (1-2 hand fulls)
Cucumber (1/2 a large cucumber)
Mint leaves (3 leaves)
Pear (1)
Alkaline water (1/2 cup or more to desired texture)

How to:
Add all items to a blender, and pulse. Enjoy!

*Add alkaline water. makes enough for two!

Why Drink This?
START your day with greens, it's the best way to regulate blood sugar, a low glycemic way to get a sweet treat in the morning, better than coffee! This shake will have you wide awake, alert and ready to take on anything. High Iron, high fiber, lowers cholesterol, heals and soothes digestive issues, hydrating, alkalizing and helps fight cancer, diabetes and all inflammation born illness.

90 Days of Prayer

DAY 2

Stay Focused.

"Set your affection on things above, not on things on the earth."
- ***(Colossians 3:2)***

When God places something on your heart and you begin to go after it, many will not understand you. Did they understand Jesus? How about the Apostles? How about all the prophets He sent before He sent His Son to save us? NOPE. None of them were understood. What makes you think the calling over your life will be any different? You are being separated and cast out from others so that God may make in you a perfect servant for Him, not for man. In serving Him, you serve man. Surround yourself with those who may understand or are open enough to accept you and your journey, everyone else will follow.

90 Days of Prayer
DAY 3

Sometimes, when I wake up in the morning, I'm either so tired or in such a rush that my morning routine may be filled with every emotion but love. I've learned that if I'm to wake up and follow God as He intends for my day, that I must wake early and seek Him first. If I am to complain I will complain to Him, and then repent and be gracious for this day ahead. There is no good day without Him guiding me, so just like you take a few minutes to make your coffee, take a few more to communicate with the Almighty. Don't worry, He sets the time, so He'll make sure you get to work when you need to. There's nothing that He won't hold up just to hear your voice.

Seek Him First.

"You, God, are my God, earnestly I seek you; I thirst for you, my whole being longs for you, in a dry and parched land where there is no water" - **(Psalm 63:1)**

90 Days of Prayer

DAY 4

Prayer Plans Your Purpose.

"But Jesus often withdrew to lonely places and prayed" - ***(Luke 5:6)***

If God is nudging you to spend more time with Him, it is because He needs time to mold you before the next step. This is the part where discipline and patience come in... You may feel ready to take on the world... But God has conquered the world..He knows best, stay close to Him through prayer... If you are frustrated...Tell Him. If you are annoyed and tired... Tell Him. You will soon feel grace fall upon you.

90 Days of Prayer

DAY 5

Remember Your Purpose.

*"Do not be conformed to this world, but be transformed by the renewal of your mind, that by testing you may discern what is the will of God, what is good and acceptable and perfect." - **(Romans 12:2)***

A lot of times we get consumed by power, money and the physical world....We forget why we have it. God gives power to those who serve Him. If you forget whom you serve, everything will be taken from you, for you are no longer serving your purpose. Take heed to pray often and communicate in God's Will for your life so that He may make "straight YOUR path."

One sin leads to another. Learn from those who came before us. David, Saul, Samson and all the many others to whom much power was given, but so many times they forgot who gave it to them and for what purposes.

90 Days of Prayer
DAY 6

Weakness Means There is Room for GROWTH.

*"For you, God, tested us; you refined us like silver." - **(Psalm 66:10)***

God doesn't test you in areas of which you already know how to deal... He tests you in your weakness and promotes you in your strengths.

#Praythiswithme *"Lord, God, I thank you for the tests in my life. For the anxiety, pain and for every "no" that I wished and prayed for to be a "yes." For all the people who are no longer a part of my life. For these were all a test of one thing: my TRUST in You."*

90 Days of Prayer
DAY 7

Your **Weaknesses**

*"Count it all joy, my brothers, when you meet trials of various kinds, for you know that the testing of your faith produces steadfastness. And let steadfastness have its full effect, that you may be perfect and complete, lacking in nothing." - **(James 1: 2-4)***

Tests come in the form of things that are difficult for YOU to overcome. You ever stop and wonder why you can't stop dating the wrong person? Or stop drinking, smoking, or selling yourself short? Ever wonder 'how come my friends or family members don't have the same problems as me?' It's because the test is created based on the student. Your weakness determines your test, but your faith determines your testimony. Be strong. Don't give in. This too will pass, and once you pass you will move on to the next. The tests do not get easier, you just get stronger.

Determine Your Test.

Vegan-

Recipe for Today

Ingredients:
1- Large Avocado
1 Roma Tomato
1 cucumber
5-7 Basil Leaves

How to:
Slice all ingredients, layer one on top of the other, add salt & pepper to taste.

Caprese Salad

Recipe for the week

Why Eat This?
Omega-3 Fats, cancer prevention, anti-bacterial, boosts immune system, eye care & high fiber content.

90 Days of Prayer

DAY 8

YOU **AREN'T** GOING TO CHANGE PEOPLE ON **YOUR** TIME.

*"By hearing ye shall hear, and shall not understand; and seeing ye shall see, and shall not perceive:, for this people's heart is waxed gross, and their ears are dull of hearing, and their eyes they have closed; lest at any time they should see with their eyes and hear with their ears, and should understand with their heart, and should be converted, and I should heal them." - **(Matthew 13:14-15)***

You're not going to change people on your time. Accept them for who they are. The main thing is to not become like them. Allow them their time to want to change their ways. Find peace knowing who God created you to be. People are people. They will change when they are ready to.

90 Days of Prayer
DAY 9

We Were Only Given the Will to Choose Right From Wrong, **NOT to Create It.**

"Having the understanding darkened, being alienated from the Life of God through the ignorance that is in them, because of the blindness of their heart: who being past feeling have given themselves over unto lasciviousness, to work all uncleanness with greediness."
- (Ephesians 4:18)

We were only given the will to choose right from wrong, not create it. If you think you have the right to create, you think you are God and in fact do not serve Him, but only yourself. Our society has gone so far into sin, that people who live in the light are alienated. People living in sin have no clue they are, and have been forged down so deep in their sin they can almost convince you that the way they are living is right. The only way to not get caught up in accepting everything in this physical world as "right" is to keep your eyes fixed on The CREATOR OF RIGHT FROM WRONG. He has the answers. Not us. We were only given the right to choose, not to create. If you think you have the right to create, you think you are God and in fact don't serve Him, but serve only yourself.

90 Days of Prayer
DAY 10

"Be DOERS of the Word, and not hearers only, deceiving your own selves." - (James 1:22)

You Are His hands, Eyes, Ears and Mouth...

God sends His messengers to be His words, hands, eyes and ears; His legs and His help, His love and His expression. If you choose to point a finger at one of His appointed, stop yourself, sit alone and point your finger at God. It is Him you are mad at.

Has someone ever said something to you that just really hit you in the wrong spot? You sat back and thought *'why did that hurt me so badly? Maybe it's true. Truth does hurt. But I'm mad at them for saying it! What gives them the right?'* All of us have the right... more than that, the responsibility to each other. You're not always going to like it. But the good people of this world don't give up on doing right by God.

Go DO Good Works.

90 Days of Prayer

DAY 11

Sleepless Nights? Anxiety? Your *Purpose* Is NEAR!

> *"Be sober, be vigilant; because your adversary the devil, as a roaring lion, walketh about, seeking whom he may devour."* - *(1 Peter 5:8)*

Choose to focus on what God has chosen you to do. The closer you get to serving in your purpose, the harder the devil fights for your attention. Anyone else been struggling with anxiety lately? It's because you're walking in your purpose... The devil is pissed. Keep walking, matter of fact... RUN towards God.

90 Days of Prayer

DAY 12

#PRAYTHISWITHME

*"This is the day the LORD has made. We will rejoice and be glad in it." - (**Psalm 118:24**)*

Lord, I have tried, time and time again to live fully in your presence. I am sorry for my attitude, my constant unhappiness in this world. I want to take this moment to say THANK YOU for the life you have given me. To ask You to guard my thoughts and actions as I know the evil one is always trying to get me down. I KNOW that a sure sign of Your children is JOY, You teach us so much about joy and yet, we are constantly pushing it away.. Hold me close to You and hang tight to my hand even when I let go of Yours.. I need You even when I don't know to ask... Don't leave me. Amen."

90 Days of Prayer
DAY 13

#PRAYTHISWITHME
-My Marriage-

"Wives, submit to your own husbands, as to the Lord. For the husband is the head of the wife even as Christ is the head of the church, his body, and is himself its Savior. Now as the church submits to Christ, so also wives should submit in everything to their husbands. Husbands, love your wives, as Christ loved the church and gave himself up for her, that he might sanctify her, having cleansed her by the washing of water with the word" - **(Ephesians 5: 22-33)**

"Lord, I come to you and offer THANKSGIVING for my marriage, as difficult as it has been, as beautiful as it has been. Open the eyes of my heart and the heart of my husband/wife. I want to make this work. And Lord, If it is YOUR WILL, Please help us to make this work. Give him the courage to seek you in order to help us. The man should be guiding this family, and Lord, if he doesn't know how, show him, send him someone to teach him, Lord, you know my faults, and I'm sorry for them. You know my heart and I'm grateful for your intercessions, I want what you want. Teach me to be at peace when you remove certain things or people in my path to your purpose for my life... Allow me peace to accept my cross to keep certain things and people in my life. I desire what you desire for me and my family. Show me your ways... And teach me to follow them all of my days. Amen."

90 Days of Prayer
DAY 14

#PRAYTHISWITHME
-My Sickness-

" O LORD my God, I cried out to You, And You healed me" - ***(Psalm 30:2)***

"Lord, we pray for understanding and the ability to find the words to be grateful through any storm ahead of us. Teach us the lesson through our pain Lord, it is all in Your will, and we are grateful to learn. Life is easily lived and floated upon when there are no issues. I pray to conquer and defeat evil thoughts with the smallest whisper of your name. I praise you in this storm. Thank you for never leaving my side. Amen."

Recipe for the week
"Use It All" Stir-Fry

Ingredients:

- Olive Oil
- Garlic Cloves (3)
- Coconut Aminos
- Cooked Quinoa
- Cilantro
- Slivered almonds
- Sesame Seeds
- Ginger Powder
- Turmeric Powder
- Cayenne Powder
- Real Salt
- Pepper
- Zucchini
- Bell Peppers (Red/Green/Yellow)
- Mushrooms
- Cabbage (Green/White)
- Red Onion x Scallions
- Carrots

How to:
Add olive oil to hot pan, sauté all veggies, in a separate bowl, mix together all spices and coconut aminos(soy sauce substitute) and add on top of veggies, turn off the heat and serve over a bed of rice, quinoa or your favorite pasta!

Why Eat This?
Omega-3 Fats, cancer prevention, anti-bacterial, boosts immune system, eye care & high fiber content.

90 Days of Prayer

DAY 15

#PRAYTHISWITHME

"And we know that God causes everything to work together for the good of those who love God and are called according to his purpose for them." - **(Romans 8:28)**

"Lord God, God of wonders and miracles, I pray that through my pain you show me your purpose, I release myself solely into your arms of healing and hope! Send me your angels to keep me strong as I go through this stormy season. I love you and cannot wait to see what you will use my pain for... You turn all things into your good, use me Lord Jesus, in everything. Amen."

90 Days of Prayer

DAY 16

#PRAYTHISWITHME
-Motivation-

*"For those who live according to the flesh set their minds on the things of the flesh, but those who live according to the Spirit set their minds on the things of the Spirit." - **(Romans 8:5)***

"Lord, God I pray to have the strength and motivation that only you can give me to move forward in your great purpose for me. I love you and thank you in advance for keeping me focused and reminding me that I have greatness inside of me that you have instilled and even more so that you are so powerful you can curb any harm or distraction coming my way, keep me in your arms Lord God, Amen."

90 Days of Prayer
DAY 17

#PRAYTHISWITHME

"But when they shall deliver you up, take no thought how or what to speak: for it shall be given you in that hour what to speak." - **(Matthew 10:19)**

"Lord God I'm here... And I love you and I know that doesn't seem like much, but to you Lord, it is EVERYTHING. I pray that even if I don't always know what to say, you look into my heart Lord and hear the deepest pains and joys there within. I love you so much Lord and I just thought you should hear it from my lips... Help my words to match my actions in faith and love in you. Amen."

90 Days of Prayer

DAY 18

#PRAYTHISWITHME
-Your WILL over my WANT-

"In all things give thanks; for this is the will of God in Christ Jesus concerning you all."

- ***(1 Thessalonians 5:18)***

"Lord God I Pray for the grace to leave any and all situations that do not SERVE YOU, for serving you I am serving my family. I pray for the courage to put my kids before my needs. I pray for the peace to forgive those that hurt me and the courage and patience to talk with my daughter about the things she needs to say most to me. I pray for patience to hear the things that may hurt me most. I pray for my son, that I can be the mother he needs, the one he comes to and explains his pain.... I pray for forgiveness in my past. I pray and say thank you for guiding, loving and understanding. Amen."

90 Days of Prayer

DAY 19

*"Be sober, be vigilant; because your adversary the devil, as a roaring lion, walketh about, seeking whom he may devour." -(**1 Peter 5:8**)*

Do Not Wait on the Works of Evil, **Continue Doing Good.**

Our culture has a tendency to watch and wait in fear or anticipation of what someone else is going to do next. Are they going to try to break up your relationship? Get you fired? Talk bad about you? Look better than you? Lie about you? Rather than stalk their life to play defense to what is coming from them.... Get out there! Your works and purpose driven life should have them guessing at all times! Your steps have been ordained. Act like it. Let the devil wake and wonder and fear your steps. Like Scar feared Mufassa. Evil must fear good. God set it up that way. Stop living the opposite.

90 Days of Prayer

DAY 20

PRAISE HIM IN THE STORM.

"Suddenly, a fierce storm struck the lake, with waves breaking into the boat. But Jesus was sleeping. The disciples went and woke him up, shouting, "Lord, save us! We're going to drown!" He replied, "You of little faith, why are you so afraid?" Then he got up and rebuked the winds and the waves, and it was completely calm."" -*(Matthew 8:24-26)*

At night, I notice, when my body and mind are finally sitting to relax... The evil one attacks. Why? Because he knows I need sleep to get up the next day and do God's work.... Or do I? He has tested me night after night.... And I've learned to THANK God for allowing this testing. For it has made me trust in Him for strength and energy... Not the amount of sleep I get. And sure enough, I thank God in the midst of trial, and He allows me to sleep peacefully and wake with energy for all of His work ahead. Defeat evil with praise to God. Praise Him always!

Tabouli Cups

Recipe for the week

Ingredients:

Parsley (1 Bunch)
Tomato (2)
Green bell pepper(1)
Green onion(1/2 bunch)
Bulgar wheat (coarsely ground, 2-3 tbsp)
Lemon (1/4 cup)
Real Salt (to taste)
Pepper(to taste)
Olive Oil (Extra Virgin 3 tbsp)
Mint leaves (3-5)
Cabbage or Lettuce (1 head)
*** Preferably Organic Ingredients.

How to:

Finely chop all ingredients and add to large bowl. Add lemon, olive oil and spices. Mix together and spoon into cabbage or lettuce cups, serve!

Why Eat This?

Liver, bloodstream and colon cleanse. Anti-inflammatory, antioxidant, full of fiber & Vitamin C and a nutrition powerhouse!

90 Days of Prayer

DAY 21

USE

*"Each of you should use whatever gift you have received to serve others, as faithful stewards of God's grace in its various forms." - **(1 Peter 4:10)***

EVERY

Thank You Lord, for choosing me. I can't wait to get out of bed and serve You and Your people! God chose ME!!! What a blessing! Go use every ounce of talent and drive and charm and beauty and joy and intelligence in His love!!

BLESSING.

90 Days of Prayer

DAY 22

Do Not Worry.

*""Therefore I tell you, do not worry about your life, what you will eat or drink; or about your body, what you will wear. Is not life more than food, and the body more than clothes? Look at the birds of the air; they do not sow or reap or store away in barns, and yet your heavenly Father feeds them. Are you not much more valuable than they? Can any one of you by worrying add a single hour to your life?" - (**Matthew 6:25-27**)*

Do not worry about what is coming next. Your main concern is in the now. Pray to think this way: "How can I be the best example of God's love right now where I'm at? How can I be used as a vessel for Him?" Let Him worry about tomorrow. He has already gone before you. Everyday I wake up, regardless of how terrible the day before was or how terrifying the day ahead will be. I say "thank you Lord for choosing me." It makes all anger, sleeplessness and lack of courage disappear.

90 Days of Prayer

DAY 23

*"He that is patient, is governed with much wisdom: but he that is impatient, exalteth his folly." - **(Proverbs 14:29)***

Sometimes, life is just about waiting until tomorrow to receive the blessing you wanted today. Trusting God to guide your steps daily. In His time, not yours.

Patience.

90 Days of Prayer

DAY 24

Walking...

> "Thy word is a lamp unto my feet, and a light unto my path."
>
> - **(Psalm 119:105)**

Anyone who has ever accomplished anything great for mankind did it alone. It wasn't until after the success, that they had supporters. Remember when you're in battle, God walks with you. You are not alone. Lean on Him. Shrug off the haters and those jealous of the favor on your life... Your focus is on the one giving you favor.

Alone.

90 Days of Prayer
DAY 25

Growing Pains

""And we know that to them that love God, all things work together unto good, to such as, according to his purpose, are called to be saints" - (**Romans 8:28**)

Growing pains are God's way of teaching us. Anytime you struggle with physical pain, emotional distress or psychological anxiety, know that God will use these things for His glory if you let Him. There is a lesson in it. Be open to the lesson and shut the door to impatience and frustration. Pray as hard as you work to find purpose in your trials.

90 Days of Prayer

DAY 26

Bless Those Who Work Hard.

If you aren't willing to be patient, work hard and develop the life God set for you, don't be mad at those who do.

"The soul of the sluggard craves and gets nothing, while the soul of the diligent is richly supplied."

- **(Proverbs 13:14)**

90 Days of Prayer

DAY 27

WE ALL HAVE A CHOICE

"Husbands, love your wives, as Christ also loved the church, and delivered himself up for it: That he might sanctify it, cleansing it by the laver of water in the word of life:

That he might present it to himself a glorious church, not having spot or wrinkle, or any such thing; but that it should be holy, and without blemish. So also ought men to love their wives as their own bodies. He that loveth his wife, loveth himself." - **(Ephesians 5:25-28)**

People are people. They sin. They hurt others. I want a husband who can withstand the tests of sin not because he loves me, but because he loves God so much that sinning against me, a gift from God to him, would be betraying God's love.

90 Days of Prayer

DAY 28

FAITH AND FOOD

*"And God said, "Behold, I have given you every plant yielding seed that is on the face of all the earth, and every tree with seed in its fruit. You shall have them for food." - **(Genesis 1:29)***

Food has so much to do with our physiological state. You eat clean, you think clean and feel clean. You eat foods dipped in chemicals, altered at their genetic state, and expect to not have a deficiency? God intended for food to help and heal us. Not to harm us.

Recipe for the week

Spicy Hummus Dip

Ingredients:
- Garbanzo beans (1 cup)
- Sesame tahini (1/2 cup)
- Lemon (1/3 cup)
- Garlic clove (1-2 large)
- Real salt (to taste)
- Pepper (to taste)
- Cayenne pepper (to taste)

*** Preferably Organic Ingredients.

How to:
Add everything into a food processor and pulse until creamy!

Why Eat This?
High fiber, high protein, anti-bacterial, anti-inflammatory, antioxidants, heart healthy, promotes good digestion and intestinal health.

90 Days of Prayer

DAY 29

"And let us not grow weary while doing good, for in due season we shall reap if we do not lose heart."

- *(Galatians 6:9)*

GOD USES YOU.

Even those you never intended on inspiring are moved by you being YOU. Allowing God to flow freely in and out of your words, actions and lifestyle moves others.... Never stop being the you God created you to be. You're saving lives daily.

90 Days of Prayer

DAY 30

"For my thoughts are not your thoughts, neither are your ways my ways, declares the LORD."

- (Genesis 15:20)

Get back on track. Stay Focused. Stay Disciplined. Have Passion. Thank Him for all of your setbacks. They are setting you up for something you cannot have ever imagine!!! When you notice a set back, praise Him, relax in the notion that He is taking the wheel and showing you a new way; changing you, stay focused on His will.

Stay Focused.

90 Days of Prayer

DAY 31

God's Perspective

I always wonder about God's perspective. For example, when we're sitting in the car driving somewhere we don't want to go, maybe we hate our job, or maybe we hate the people we have to be around, or maybe we're struggling to go home because our family situation is rough. You're crying tears in the car while you're angry and you're frustrated and you're headed to your destination and God seeing you from Heaven, is smiling, not because you're miserable, but because you haven't given up on Him in your hardest time and He sees what is coming in your future. So as you were driving along miserably He was watching you get to your purpose! Your destination may just be around that corner.... If you could just get there.

"Not that I have already obtained this or am already perfect, but I press on to make it my own, because Christ Jesus has made me his own.."

- (Philippans 3:12)

90 Days of Prayer

DAY 32

God Loves You the Way You Are and Also Loves You Enough to *Not* Leave You the Way You Are.

"But God shows his love for us in that while we were still sinners, Christ died for us." - (Romans 5:8)

A lot of times we think that being loved means not having to grow, change or walk in our purpose, fully. But maybe God is calling you to change certain things in your life that are blocking your purpose and further calling He has over your life. Open your heart to the idea of change and pray for the strength to accept people God sends your way as a means of communicating that change to you on Earth. I had to learn to change, the very hard way. It wasn't until I was sick, miserable and fed up at my worst that I was open to change for the best God had in store for me. I had to let go of foods that were harming me, boyfriends and friends that were not contributing to my purpose and habits of stress and overworking myself. Let go of who you were, to become who you are.

90 Days of Prayer

DAY 33

Ask God to show you who you are. Ask God to reveal your true nature to you from an outside perspective. A lot of times, we think we are perfect, we're happy, we're unflawed, our personality is so kind-hearted that we can't imagine anything we do could hurt someone else with. However, none of us are perfect and to someone

WHO ARE YOU?

else our facial expressions, our tone and word selection can be offensive to others, and more so, hurtful, which blocks the other person from receiving you fully. Ask God to reveal you, to yourself, so you know your flaws. So you don't hurt others with them.

> *"Be completely humble and gentle; be patient, bearing with one another in love." - (Ephesians 4:2)*

90 Days of Prayer
DAY 34

Let's Talk About Love
(1 Corinthians 13: 4-8, Ephesians 5:33)

"Be completely humble and gentle; be patient, bearing with one another in love." - ***(Ephesians 4:2)***

Love is a tricky tricky thing, especially because it can be confused by lust. God has given us a guide as to how and who to love, He says : " Love is patient, love is kind. It does not envy, it does not boast, it is not proud. It does not dishonor others, it is not self-seeking, it is not easily angered, it keeps no record of wrongs. Love does not delight in evil but rejoices with the truth. It always protects, always trusts, always hopes, always perseveres." He continues, "However, let each one of you love his wife as himself, and let the wife see that she respects her husband." I've learned to live this way, the man I allow to love me and have my heart, the man that God has chosen for me has to want to love, care and appreciate me in action and word on his own, without guidance from me. That desire must come from God inside of his heart. The changes God needs to make in him before me must happen without me. Just as God makes changes in me before sending me to him, so that we can grow together when we get to that point.

Recipe for the week

Carrot - Apple Juice

How to:
You will need a juicer. Place all items in juicer seperately, add some water to desired texture.

Ingredients:
Organic Carrots (4)

Organic Red Delicious Apples (1)

Organic Ginger Root (1/2 in.)

Why Eat This?
Cancer fighting, Immune boosting, anti-inflamatory, full of antioxidants. Great for fighting off flus and colds!

90 Days of Prayer

DAY 35

*" For God hath not given us the spirit of fear; but of power, and of love, and of a sound mind." - **(2 Timothy 1:7)***

On *Relationships.*

I want you to know that I am afraid. I've been hurt by men I've dated most of my life and honestly I feel and felt like God must have wanted me to be alone because it has never worked out. I'm tired of being hurt and it's hard for me to let that go, but I'm praying about it and I want to conquer this fear and anxiety about relationships. I put so much pressure on "what if it doesn't work" or "what if he isn't the right one?" That sometimes I'm too afraid to try. But I do want to change. I hate fear. I hate giving the devil an "in". I'm shutting that door today.

90 Days of Prayer

DAY 36

When you ask God to help you with something, expect to be tested by it, but also expect to come to God, bring this issue to His feet and for Him to give you an answer to solve it. If you do this, and fail over and over again to move past the issue, come back until you hear the voice of God in the form of grace and a solution to your problem. He is training you to depend on Him during the storm. You don't have all of the answers. And as I grow, I'm learning, I have none of the answers. The foot of The Cross does. How much time are you spending there?

Training day.

*"For bodily exercise is profitable to little: but godliness is profitable to all things, having promise of the life that now is, and of that which is to come." - **(1 Timothy 4:8)***

90 Days of Prayer
DAY 37

Your calling, Your Service

"The spirit of truth, whom the world cannot receive, because it seeth him not, nor knoweth him: but you shall know him; because he shall abide with you, and shall be in you."

- (John 14:17)

You may not be able to see what evil is doing or plotting against you, but God does. He sees all the bad and immoral plots against you and all of His children and He may be calling YOU to fix it. Don't brush off the call, or think someone else will do it... If not you, then who? Your calling, your service. Spend time in prayer, praying away the attempts of the enemy. All battles need strategy, even spiritual ones. I don't know about you, but I always feel at a disadvantage because i cannot see what my enemy can, but with prayer, and the gift of The Holy Spirit, we are always on the winning team, we may slip for a while, but until we learn to fight in prayer we will never fully see the glory of God. Leave your battles, at the pew, at the Foot of The Cross. Give them all to God, in specifics, do not let your prayer time be vague, your needs and your struggles are not vague, they are detailed and specific.... watch Him fight for you and give you the authority, patience and love to fight some of your battles on His behalf. He will train you to rely on Him so that next time? You will be the One He calls to go out on His behalf with His Spirit to help another.

90 Days of Prayer

DAY 38

Wait

Ladies, when dating or marrying, wait for someone you can be honest with. Someone you can be honest with about your faults, areas you need help growing in and insecurities. I never thought I could be honest. I was always told 'it wouldn't work' but as I grow in Christ, I'm learning that the best way to live is honestly and unapologetically for who God has molded you to be and the method HE has chosen to do it in. The person He sends you, will not only accept that, but encourage you to keep going.

What Do You Have to Lose?

"I wait for the LORD, my soul waits, and in his word I hope; my soul waits for the Lord more than watchmen for the morning, more than watchmen for the morning." - **(Psalms 130:5-6)**

90 Days of Prayer
DAY 39

Fears, Lies and Guilt...

"The thief comes only to steal, kill and destroy, I have come that they may have life, and have it to the full."
- ***(John 10:10)***

The devil will always come in the form of a lie, guilt, fear or manipulation of your heart. When you see ANY of these signs from people or situations, know it is him. And know there is hope because God has already conquered the world. This is no new event or situation for Him, look that demon in the eyes and say "I serve Jesus Christ the Almighty and powerful God, and the Holy Spirit guides me, I want nothing to do with you, I have already chosen my team, be GONE, in the name of Jesus Christ The Lord!" There is nothing the enemy hates more than the name of Jesus. Many ask me " Diana, how do you get past your fears or pain? I tell them whenever anxiety hits me I say the Mighty Name of Jesus! "Jesus, I need You." (Repeat 3 times, and say daily or hourly or by the minute as needed.)

Oh My!

90 Days of Prayer
DAY 40

FILLING VOIDS

"Why do you spend money for what is not bread, And your wages for what does not satisfy? Listen carefully to Me, and eat what is good, And delight yourself in abundance." - **(Isaiah 55:2)**

After you've dyed your hair red, black, put highlights in it, chopped it off, changed your room around, bought a new wardrobe, cleaned out your closet, dumped your boyfriend in search of another and left your job… Only to find yourself unchanged, and still a void exists. You'll end up like me, sitting and praying that God hears you, that maybe He hears the plea of your tiny little heart amongst all the others in your true and utter unhappiness. And one day, you'll realize that all of those things won't bring neither change nor happiness….But God, by design, created us to crave Him…And without Him we will never change nor fill our voids.

90 Days of Prayer

DAY 41

Are You Being Called?

*"But you, take courage! Do not let your hands be weak, for your work shall be rewarded." - **(2 Chronicles 15:7)***

There are many courageous lives that we celebrate throughout our calendar year and many have shaped the life we live today. Jesus, being the first, but because our Lord and Savior came to teach us, many have followed in His steps, (as we were asked to do by our Heavenly Father.) He has been a guiding light for many that came after, Dr. Martin Luther King Jr... being one of them. The greatest thing MLK JR. DID was NOT GIVE IN OR UP. HE kept going. He knew God's mission was not a bargain or a trade or a "meet me half way" conversation. He knew what God had asked of him, and he kept going. Will you?

Recipe for the week

"Buns" Ingredients:

1 cup cooked quinoa

1/2 cup quinoa flour

1/2 cup water

Real Salt

Garlic powder

Black pepper

**spices to taste

How to:

Mix together all ingredients in a bowl, and you can make the 'buns' on a skillet, pan or even in a waffle maker! It's up to you! Cook until crispy on the outside!

Why Eat This?

High protein, gluten free, high fiber, blood cleansing, great for digestion, anti-inflammatory, low glycemic (great for diabetics) high omega-3 fats.

Falafelburger

To Make Falafel Patties See Page 110

"Spicy Mayo" Ingredients:

cayenne
lemon
real Salt
black pepper
sesame Tahini
water
garlic Powder

How to:

Add cayenne, lemon, garlic powder, Real Salt and black pepper into a small bowl, add 1/2 tbsp sesame tahini and a few drops of water and mix until creamy in texture.

90 Days of Prayer

DAY 42

Be Uncomfortable.

Force yourself to be uncomfortable and acknowledge the things that have been hindering you from peace and happiness. If you can be that uncomfortably honest with God just one time, watch what He will reveal to you. Anytime i find myself getting too comfortable with my life and the road is too smooth, I know I am no threat to the enemy and his plans. When I can live in the peace of Christ in the midst of madness that's how I know I am walking in His will regardless of the enemy's plot against me. Be joyous in discomfort!

> *"Seeing the crowds, he went up on the mountain, and when he sat down, his disciples came to him. And he opened his mouth and taught them, saying: "Blessed are the poor in spirit, for theirs is the kingdom of heaven. "Blessed are those who mourn, for they shall be comforted. "Blessed are the meek, for they shall inherit the earth..." - **(Matthew 5:1-48)***

90 Days of Prayer
DAY 43

TOLERANCE.

"Surely I have calmed and quieted my soul, Like a weaned child with his mother; Like a weaned child is my soul within me." - (Psalm 131:2)

There are so many forces trying to split you apart from the things and people you love. The evil one works to DIVIDE. But you can WIN. Calm yourself and ask God why stress and anxiety and fear take over as a natural means of "coping" with something or someone. God will teach you PEACE in the midst of any situation. Stop running away from everything and Put your foot down, do not tolerate words that bring you down, do not tolerate manipulative situations. But rather bring them all to God. He will give you vision and discernment on how to remove anxiety, and replace it with understanding, forgiveness and love. Those 3, they can cure anything.

90 Days of Prayer
DAY 44

YOU ARE WOR-THY.

" Don't worry about anything; instead, pray about everything. Tell God what you need, and thank him for all he has done. Then you will experience God's peace, which exceeds anything we can understand. His peace will guard your hearts and minds as you live in Christ Jesus."

- (Philippians 4:6-7)

You may not feel worthy or good enough for someone or something but if God does, it will be yours. You see, God is working on you just as much as He is working on what He has FOR you. Your destination is waiting for you and you don't even know what it is yet, and it doesn't know it needs you until it receives you. Don't hold back. Go for it. God is guiding you!

90 Days of Prayer

DAY 45

YOUR DESIRES ARE INTENTIONAL!

"Pray that the LORD your God will tell us where we should go and what we should do."
- (Philippians 4:6-7)

Trust that God knows what you desire most because guess who put those desires there? He DID!!! He knows your strengths and weaknesses. He gave them BOTH to you... Allow Him to work in your life and the lives of those around you in your favor for His glory!

90 Days of Prayer
DAY 46

THE GIFT OF

"Behold I send you as sheep in the midst of wolves. Be ye therefore wise as serpents and harmless as doves." - **(Matthew 10:16)**

God will give you discernment to see who is playing on His team and who has sold their jersey to play for the opposition. Use wisdom when addressed by these people. They will try to manipulate your mind and are snake like with their words. Remain still. Don't prepare your conversations but wait on the Lord for your responses.

DISCERNMENT.

90 Days of Prayer

DAY 47

ENOUGH IS NEVER ENOUGH FOR SOMEONE **DRIVEN BY MONEY.**

"No one can serve two masters. For you will hate one and love the other; you will be devoted to one and despise the other. You cannot serve both God and money."

- (Matthew 6:24)

The love of anything materialistic is a funny thing. You see, people who chase it, never have enough. Just when they think they do, they don't again. Be grateful. The little I have is plenty for me! Choosing joy in Christ means choosing an everlasting joy, not a temporary one. Money, fame, lust, greed are all temporary fixes to an eternal thirst for Christ. Never trade your morals for money. That's when you lose who you are in Christ.

90 Days of Prayer

DAY 48

DON'T Doubt Your Journey.

*"And everyone will hate you because you are my followers. But the one who endures to the end will be saved." - **(Matthew 6:24)***

Some people have so much insecurity, all they can do is bash you for conquering yours. Remind yourself that people's sarcasm and condescending ways are YEARS of psychological damage caused by their environment. It can be broken!!! Love and encouragement can fix even the worst case. Those who are joyous, feel they can accomplish anything in Christ and don't doubt their journey are those who love God enough to trust Him to see them through. Be a light in a dark situation, guiding others to see what you see in Christ.

Garlic Herb Dressing:
Organic olive oil (1tsp)
Lemon juice (1 tbsp)
Apple cider vinegar (1tsp)
Dried Italian seasoning blend
Real salt
Black pepper
Garlic powder
(All seasoning to taste)

Diana's EPIC Salad Recipe!

Recipe for the week

Ingredients:

Romaine Lettuce
Spinach
Kale
Tomato
Cucumber
Avocado
Carrot
Yams
Pumpkin Seeds
Sunflower Seeds
Red Onion
Garbanzo Beans
Olives (optional)
*** Preferably all organic produce.

How to:

Wash and chop all ingredients, add to bowl. Add as much of each as suits you or those you are feeding. I like to roast my seeds in a pan, on medium, with a little coconut oil and Real Salt.(Or you can use them raw, it's totally up to you.)

Why Eat This?

High fiber, high protein, anti-bacterial, anti-inflammatory, antioxidants, heart healthy, promotes good digestion and intestinal health.

90 Days of Prayer

DAY 49

BEING GOD'S CHILD

It wasn't until I found God that I found and respected myself. It wasn't until that happened that I found realized HOW to wait on God's timing to work in a man and work in me separately before we could meet and recognize one another. Ladies, what you put out is a lot of the time what you get back in return. Being single isn't a curse, it's a blessing to be God's child. And wait on His timing and who He is preparing for you. I always say, "I'd rather have no company than the wrong company." Wait on God's great company. Wait.

> *"There is a time for everything, and a season for every activity under the heavens." - (Ecclesiastes 3:1)*

90 Days of Prayer
DAY 50

NOT HEARING THE **CALLING?**

*""And it came to pass in those days, that he went out into a mountain to pray, and he passed the whole night in the prayer of God." - **(Luke 6:12)***

God is still (without movement) in your life, it is quiet and you feel like you're not hearing the calling over your life. This is the time to rejoice! This is time in your training, God is molding and shaping you! Remember you are in transition. Transitioning from level to level requires spending time in silence waiting on God's Word and next move not your own. There's a reason Jesus kept going to the mountain away from the world to be with His Father, if Jesus had to be quiet and wait on The Word from the Mouth of God, you most definitely should too. The Word of God is coming to you and your mission is before you! Stay focused. Stay in prayer. And follow His lead.

90 Days of Prayer
DAY 51

Attitude OF Gratitude

"Jesus said to the woman, "Your faith has saved you; go in peace." - ***(Luke 7:50)***

Thank you Lord for the moments we hit a low in life and think we're being punished. It is actually in those moments that God brings out purpose and understanding of many situations we didn't see before. I remember a few months after being diagnosed with my ovarian tumor, I started thanking God for my sickness. You may think that sounds weird, but I got to a point in my walk with Christ, that I wanted Him to know that I was truly thankful for the pain, because of that pain I was getting closer and closer to Christ. Pain brought me purpose. In my pain I was learning what He was asking of me. I learned to praise Him in the storm. It must get worse before it gets better, but when it gets better, your faith will be what saved you.

90 Days of Prayer

DAY 52

"The Lord will fight for you; you need only to be still." - (Exodus 14:14)

God is

Last night before bed I was telling my mom how stressed I felt, a lot going on in my life and me feeling like the burden is too great. She reminded me that it's because I was trying to carry to load....And to give it to God and trust

FIGHTING

Him to provide. When it feels like the weight of the world is too heavy a burden to carry, it's because it is. You were not created to carry it, give it to God. Stop trying to fight your own battles. He will fight them for you.

FOR YOU!

90 Days of Prayer

DAY 53

CROSS THROUGH THE STORM

*"Immediately He made the disciples get into the boat and go ahead of Him to the other side, while He sent the crowds away." - **(Matthew 14:22)***

Lord, I am patient. I am your servant. I will not be moved. Although, the storms in my life are rough, and although I cry myself to sleep, I will not let evil win, I will not succumb to the pressure of believing you aren't My Savior, my Healer and my Refuge! I know You are here and will show yourself in the ways you deem appropriate and I will wait for your timing over mine. Thank you for the blessings I see and especially for those I don't see. I remember the scene with Peter in the boat and right before Jesus asked him to step off the boat, he had to remind the crew (who wanted to go back because they were afraid of the severity of the storm) on the boat that Jesus "wants us to pass through the storm!" You see, Jesus could have halted the storm to allow Peter to walk off the boat gracefully, but that WASN'T the plan! The plan was for Peter to TRUST what God said. He said to cross through the storm and He would meet them on the other side, so Peter made sure his friends listened and followed.

90 Days of Prayer
DAY 54

GOD FILLS VOIDS,

"O God, you are my God; early will I seek you: my soul thirsts for you, my flesh longs for you in a dry and thirsty land, where no water is;" - **(Psalm 63:1)**

Sometimes, the hardest lessons to learn are those you need to learn the most. One for me, has been learning that ONLY God can fill voids. People can't. The moment you let yourself trust that someone; whether man or woman can fill the place God should be in your life, is the moment you will realize how foolish that idea is. No one can fill the giant gaping hole inside of you, only God can. He designed us to desire Him. Desire Him above anyone or anything else, and you shall be whole. I know this to be true because I have messed up so many times, and have been let down by the very people I never thought I'd be let down by. **NOT PEOPLE.**

Recipe for the week

Garlic-Tahini Sauce

How to:
Mix until smooth in texture. Add water if necessary for texture.

Ingredients:
2 tbsp Sesami Tahini

4 tbsp Lemon Juice

1 tsp Real Salt

1 tsp Garlic Powder

Why Eat This?
Great for digestion, anti-bacterial, antiviral, vitamin C, Iron, Calcium & high fiber.

90 Days of Prayer
DAY 55

"I will strengthen you and help you; I will uphold you with my righteous right hand." - **(Isaiah 41:10)**

When you are feeling loss, sadness, remorse or hurt. Turn to the one who knows these all too well. He lost His only Son, He is saddened by the sins of the world, He feels remorse for those who are troubled in fear and hurting for those whose pain is too great. He is near to the sorrowful, His strength is made perfect in our weakness. He is our redeeming grace, our painful purpose and our righteous and joyous Savior!

FEELING LOSS.

90 Days of Prayer
DAY 56

"This is the day the LORD has made; We will rejoice and be glad in it.." - **(Psalm 118:24)**

I DARE YOU

It's very easy to focus on the doings of evil in your life. It's easy to moan and groan and complain and gossip and take your anger out with your negative words on the world. You know what's hard? Gratitude. Having the grace to be thankful in the midst of all that is going wrong, to focus on what is and what can be going right! I dare you to focus on it! I double-dog-dare YOU! I decree and declare a dare, that you, yes you, will not complain today about how little sleep you got, the argument you and your favorite person got into, the emotional state you are in, the amount of work you have to do, the pains in your body, the amount of money you make, the pains in your heart, or anything else.

90 Days of Prayer
DAY 57

PUT THE **BEST** IN.

"Fruit trees of all kinds will grow on both banks of the river. Their leaves will not wither, nor will their fruit fail. Every month they will bear fruit, because the water from the sanctuary flows to them. Their fruit will serve for food and their leaves for healing." - **(Psalm 118:24)**

Put the best in so you can push the rest out. That's with anything in life: food, family, friends, the company you keep, your job, your passions, your thoughts and your ideas. I was speaking at a health food store about the importance of taking care of your body and I remembered the saying "put the best in so you can push the rest out." Put the best food in your temple. It will push out the toxins and the bad that's in there. Put in the best attitude, it will bring out the bad attitude. Put your best foot forward in all circumstances, it will push out the worst. What will you put in today?

90 Days of Prayer
DAY 58

"The LORD'S loving kindnesses indeed never cease, For His compassions never fail." - ***(Lamentations 3:22)***

Sensitive

Being sensitive is not an issue. Being sensitive is how you meet the needs of others. It's what makes us human and not animals or worst... robots. But when being sensitive takes over your life in a way that you cannot function, where you are almost handicapped by your emotional state, and that is where the issue comes into play. Use your emotions to help you and help God's children. Jesus was extremely sensitive to the needs of others, He could feel what everyone needed and innately, the bad things going on around Him were being shown to Him by God, so He was extremely sensitive to the Word of the Lord, to the next step, to the greater good. Being sensitive to the right matters, is a great gift indeed! Do not be afraid to be sensitive. Be afraid to feel nothing at all, it is then, that hope is lost.

90 Days of Prayer

DAY 59

GROWING

*"Come to Me all you who are heavy burdened and I shall give you rest." - **(Lamentations 3:22)***

God bless the growth process. It is where warriors are made and Saints are equipped. Your mind is the battlefield. Your flesh is the enemy's target. But your spirit is the life force in which you fight. Prayer is your weapon of choice and scriptures are your arsenal. Let Him fight for you. Let Him provide you rest during this process of trials, tribulations and testing. We all go through it, together, separately and differently. There is only growth when we are being stretched spiritually, and during this stretch, it will be painful. It is hard to look at yourself and constantly feel the tug of Christ purging and removing things in your character that hinder your growth in Him. He will remove things you do in the flesh that keep you from Him, and He will remove unforgiveness, people, jobs, thoughts etc. Allow Him to work all of these things out of you. Give Him permission. He won't do it without your obedience and acceptance. We serve a God Who is a gentleman, He knocks before entering your life. You will be all the better for it.

P A I N S .

90 Days of Prayer
DAY 60

PRAY FOR ME

""Do nothing from selfishness or empty conceit, but with humility of mind regard one another as more important than yourselves; do not merely look out for your own personal interests, but also for the interests of others."
- ***(Philippians 2:3-4)***

Keep God's people around you. What I mean by that is, when you are going through the storms of your life, you need people who pray for you so that God can answer you through them. God speaks through us! Yes US!!! They will encourage you to keep going because God has a purpose in your pain. They will offer you the one thing greater than anything else, prayer. Praying for someone is the strongest form of love available. That is a way of showing someone you care for them, not just telling them. Who have you prayed for today?

90 Days of Prayer
DAY 61

You Are Who You Hang Out With

"The Pharisees saw this and said to his disciples, "Why does your teacher eat with tax collectors and sinners?" He heard this and said, "Those who are well do not need a physician, but the sick do." - ***(Matthew 9:11-12)***

You hear that saying often right? Jesus was spending His time with the sinners of the world. He, himself, came "I have not come to call the righteous, but sinners to repentance." (Luke 5:32) But in reality, Jesus was not who He spent time with, He was the one to change them, save them and redeem them. If you are to spend time with those who are living in sin, make sure to be the light in their lives. Do not let their sin, become your sin. Ask Jesus to guide you in your steps to live as He did and help those around you, like He did.

90 Days of Prayer

DAY 62

You Don't Need to Control Everything

"Therefore do not be anxious about tomorrow, for tomorrow will be anxious for itself. Sufficient for the day is its own trouble." - (Matthew 6:34)

Some people are numb to the voice of God and His direction, because their own voice controls that of Gods. Control, we want it, in every aspect of our lives. Emotionally, we want to subdue our feelings and feel "in control" of them. Physically, we want to look how society claims for us to look and want to look like we have " self control" when it comes to our appearance. With our relationships and jobs, it's always a "power struggle" to see who ends up on top, who has the last word, and who is "the boss" or who "runs things." In reality, I've learned the less I control, the more I receive. God has promised us so much, but if we cannot relinquish control and the need to have it, we will never be able to fully hear the word of God and His direction in our lives, then we will wonder how we got so lost on our path to purpose. Let go, let God.

90 Days of Prayer

DAY 63

When Dating...

When you are dating, remember that as much as someone is changing or wants to change, that there are demons from their past and yours lurking below the surface. Those demons will come out in the means of hurtful words or actions without that person knowing what they're doing. That's how the devil wins! He brings out things from our past that we try to put away and grow from. Take up your cross as long as you

"Therefore if anyone is in Christ, he is a new creature; the old things passed away; behold, new things have come."
- (2 Corinthians 5:17)

live. Fight off the evil one by knowing how to pray him and his minions away! Pray that you don't hurt yourself or others in the process changing your old life and sins, to your new life with Christ.

90 Days of Prayer

DAY 64

Manage Your Stress

"But when you pray, go into your room, close the door and pray to your Father, who is unseen. Then your Father, who sees what is done in secret, will reward you."
- (2 Corinthians 5:17)

Managing stress is key. You can't keep running from the things that frustrate you or confuse you or take you out of your comfort zone. Share your fears with God and allow Him to work in and on you and on the things you fear most. Face them not head on in your own ways, but face them on your knees, alone in your room, at Church in a place where you can get alone with Christ and hear how He would have you manage this situation. And most of the time, you'll walk into it, fearful, but God will prove to you time and time again that He takes care of everything, all you have to do is bring it to Him and trust Him for it.

90 Days of Prayer
DAY 65

Everything Is a Spiritual Battle

""I call heaven and earth to witness against you today, that I have set before you life and death, the blessing and the curse. So choose life in order that you may live, you and your descendants."

- (Deuteronomy 30:19)

EVERYTHING. You know that moment when someone you know very well does something out of character and it confuses you? Or how about that moment when you react to say or do something totally off your good moral character? There are demons fending for our thoughts, words and actions just like God is. But, because God gave us all free will, we get to choose which is in control on any given day in any particular moment. I remember a time, I was dating a guy, and he did something so far out of his character of love and respect for me, that I told him that there are demons preying on his mind and heart and that if he let them win we would never be together. He had to choose to allow God to penetrate his heart so that he would treat me as the Child of God that I am. We all have decisions to make, which will you choose?

90 Days of Prayer
DAY 66

FILLING *Voids*

"His purpose was for the nations to seek after God and perhaps feel their way toward him and find him—though he is not far from any one of us."
- (Acts 17:27)

Filling a void? Usually the void you are filling is God. Whatever you attempt to replace Him with WILL NOT DO. As a matter of fact, it will do the opposite. Trying to forget about your problems by filling your time with bad people? I am sure that you will get into some problems you never needed. Seek Him. He will redeem and fulfill you. He makes us whole. God is love. Do not run from Him, run to Him.

Recipe for the week

Chocolate-Chip 'Nice cream'

Ingredients:
Organic ripe frozen bananas (3)
Organic cacao nibs (1/2 cup)
Cinnamon powder (to taste)
Real salt (1/4 teaspoon)
Vanilla bean powder (1 teaspoon)
Organic, nothing added, almond butter (1/2 cup)

How to:
Add all ingredients into the food processor, add water (if needed to get mixture moving in the food processor.) Once it is all combined, serve and enjoy!

Why Eat This?
High protein, high potassium, curbs appetite, high fiber, anti-inflammatory, high vitamins and antioxidants.

DAY 67

DON'T SETTLE

Sometimes people will ask you to give them "more time" and things will change. They do not specify WHAT things or who will be changing but they give you hope based on the change itself. Months or years may pass, and you will wait on this change, when in reality THEY had no intention on CHANGING but rather, waiting on you to "get used to" or settle in with whatever they have been doing. But you were not created to settle. You will push for change. Because you were created AS the change, with or without them. You see, being a creature in Christ you strive to live a righteous and holy life in His image, so anything less will compete with your Spirit, that same Spirit that dwells with The Lord. He wouldn't have that for you, nor those you love. Pursue growth in Christ, be it together or apart. Christ will always bring back together those who are truly seeking Him separately, do not fear.

> *"Enter by the narrow gate. For the gate is wide and the way is easy that leads to destruction, and those who enter by it are many. For the gate is narrow and the way is hard that leads to life, and those who find it are few."* - **(Matthew 7:13-14)**

90 Days of Prayer
DAY 68

The devil is letting out all of the stops to distract you from your purpose... But do not worry or give in to the anxiety or fear that he offers for God has something greater for you. YOU are tested BEFORE you have a testimony. If you are being attacked it is because you are on to something worth attacking. KEEP GOING. I've been under spiritual attack lately because the evil one is unhappy that I'm finally making changes that God has been asking of me. Don't be confused, those who are new to taking leaps of faith. WHEN YOU DO--- God is happy and working on your behalf, but evil is not. Evil wants you to stay complacent and miserable so that you do not progress forward in God's work. Make no mistake that God is not punishing you for taking that step...It's the evil one... Stay focused on your faith.

SPIRITUAL ATTACKS

"For God is not a God of confusion but of peace. As in all the churches of the saints." - **(1 Corinthians 14:33)**

90 Days of Prayer
DAY 69

TIME TO LEAP!

*"Therefore do not be anxious about tomorrow, for tomorrow will be anxious for itself. Sufficient for the day is its own trouble." - **(Matthew 6:34)***

You were created to do more. That decision is not up to anyone else besides God. If you are stuck, this is for you. If you are uncomfortable, this is for you. Do not ignore this. When you have outgrown where you are at, it is time to leap. Be Faith Driven. Stop making excuses to stay where you were meant to only START. You have so much waiting for you. Ask God to take your hand and walk with you as you go into the next phase of your life.

90 Days of Prayer

DAY 70

HOW OFTEN DO YOU PRAY?

"Moses was there with the LORD forty days and forty nights without eating bread or drinking water. And he wrote on the tablets the words of the covenant--the Ten Commandments." - **(Exodus 34:28)**

Prayer. Something to do in every moment. In every decision. You eat every few hours, you should pray AT LEAST that much. I need God more than I need food. He sustains me. At bare minimum a "thank you Lord." But I pray VERY often. A lot of times people have no idea that if they're in the same room with me for even a few moments that I've said a prayer in my heart. Stay in contact with God. He is constantly working on your behalf.

90 Days of Prayer

DAY 71

HE GOES BEFORE YOU.

"The LORD is the one who goes ahead of you; He will be with you. He will not fail you or forsake you. Do not fear or be dismayed."

- (Deuteronomy 31:8)

As you go through today, making tough decisions, helping those who need it and smiling through your pain...Know that God knew today was coming. He goes before you, He sees all that is coming, the good, the bad, the sad and the glad! He was on the scene much earlier than you and He will see you through all of it. Do everything to please Him, and He will do everything to protect you. God is working on your behalf... Are you working on His?

90 Days of Prayer

DAY 72

LOVE CHANGES PEOPLE

"Be shepherds of God's flock that is under your care, watching over them--not because you must, but because you are willing, as God wants you to be; not pursuing dishonest gain, but eager to serve"
- **(Deuteronomy 31:8)**

I meet so many people who complain to me about their family members and how it's frustrating to get them to change. I get it, I've been there... I'm still in there. But if there's anything I've learned is that God LOVES us into change... He doesn't force us into it. And when we do change its because WE WANT TO. Because Jesus led by example. Not because someone dragged us to it. Inspire someone to change by BEING the change. Don't talk down to others, or be negative and think that old school mentality of making fun of someone will get them to change will work. It won't. All it will do is sever ties between you and them.

NOT FORCE.

Recipe for the week

Ingredients:

1/2 cup quinoa flour

1/4 cup water

1 tsp olive oil

1 tsp garlic powder

1/4 tsp Real Salt

1/4 tsp black pepper

*I chose, hummus, avocado, spinach, tomato, olives, cucumber, red bell pepper and onions.

How to:

Mix together until thick. Pour into non stick pan (add minimum amount olive oil or coconut oil to pan if needed) cook for 5-7 min on each side until golden. Fill with whatever you'd like.

Why Eat This?

High fiber, high protein, anti-bacterial, anti-inflammatory, antioxidants, heart healthy, promotes good digestion and intestinal health.

90 Days of Prayer

DAY 73

SPEAK THE TRUTH. DO NOT EVER HOLD YOUR PEACE.

"Repent, then, and turn to God, so that your sins may be wiped out, that times of refreshing may come from the Lord."

- (Acts 3:19)

I guess my whole life and still until now, I never realized why some people are put off by me? My Mom, aka Momma Weebs, has instilled this in me... The reason being is that when I am being myself, my true, honest self, the self that is filled with Christ and His Holy Spirit, it is a reminder to others who aren't being honest, just or true, who are full of sin, unforgiveness and malice that they need now be held responsible. Is that my fault? NO. It's that, they are used to surrounding themselves with others of their same sinful nature, (not to say that I am not a sinner, because I am, but I continuously repent) Where as when they are surrounded by "yes" men... Or those who willingly lie, cheat and are deceiving.... They all blend in together. No one's actions or words hold anyone else accountable. My name is Diana Wehbe, and Jesus holds me accountable. Do you allow Him to hold you?

90 Days of Prayer

DAY 74

MAKE YOUR THOUGHTS,

"The thief comes to steal, kill and destroy, but I came that they may have life and have it to the full."
- (John 10:10)

GOD'S THOUGHTS!

Take your most negative thought, and multiply it by thousands, that is what you are up against in the world. Outside of your head. You think your thoughts are bad? Have you turned on the news lately? Heck, have you read what happened to Jesus? How they hurt Him? How Satan tested and tried Him? Mocked Him? Killed Him? Did you hear that He went through all of that for us? That His Blood would blot out our transgressions? But You can be thankful for one thing...You are thousands of steps ahead because you are thousands of prayers ahead of the world and it's ways. Your thoughts may be dark and scary, but remember we were born sinners, not Saints. We have to work at being Saints! We have authority over evil thoughts in Christ! Send those thoughts back to whom they belong to; the evil one, who is NOT you. Push out the bad thoughts... And replace them with the God thoughts.

90 Days of Prayer
DAY 75

I

"I will give thanks to You, for I am fearfully and wonderfully made; Wonderful are Your works, And my soul knows it very well.
- (Psalm 139:14)

AMA

AM

Love yourself enough to be confident in you. No matter what anyone, anywhere has to say. Because at the end of the day, there will always be someone with something to say. Remember how many good works Jesus performed here on Earth? Remember how in the midst of sickness, death and misery, Jesus performed miracle after miracle. He fulfilled Prophecy after Prophecy and yet, they mocked Him, talked badly about Him, gossiped and trashed His Name? What makes you think we're going to have it any easier? We follow Him, surely we will receive the same. He is amazing, and you? Well, when God created you, He said " it is very good," and if God thinks that, who cares what anyone else thinks? Live to please Him. Repeat to self: I am ah-mazing. I deserve the best. I love who I am.

ZING!

90 Days of Prayer

DAY 76

WHEN WAITING...

*"For God is not a God of confusion but of peace, as in all the churches of the saints.." - **(1 Corinthians 14:33)***

When things don't seem like they're working out, don't force them to. Let it go. You will soon understand why. Have Patient. When I say 'let it go' I mean, get some alone time, and literally count up all of the things you are confused about, and hand them to God. We don't serve a God of confusion, we serve a God who is organized and orderly and purposeful and intentional. So although, from our perspective it may not look like anything is moving or changing, and our prayers are going unanswered, i can promise you that is not true. God has a plan. Live each day with the intention of it being great. Change your attitude. Change your life. Let go and let God. He comes through, every time.

DOESN'T SEEM LIKE IT'S WORKING.

90 Days of Prayer
DAY 77

LET GOD CHANGE THEM, NOT YOU.

*"I will give you a new heart and put a new spirit in you; I will remove from you your heart of stone and give you a heart of flesh.." - **(Ezekiel 36:26)***

If you do not fit in my life AS YOU ARE then you do not fit. I told myself this with my ex-boyfriends. I had to learn that I am not here to change them. Same thing with friends, family and coworkers. Don't try to change anyone. If they aren't going to be what you need, they shouldn't be what you want. People grow on God's timeline, not yours. If they aren't right, right now, it doesn't mean they can't be right later. People can change. Pray for them. God will show you the way and give them the patience to hear His words of change.

90 Days of Prayer
DAY 78

A REFLECTION
A REFLECTION

> *"But I say to you, love your enemies and pray for those who persecute you"* - **(Matthew 5:44)**

Just because someone hates you, doesn't mean you can't love them. I had a coworker who bullied me constantly. I found it very difficult to pray for this person. Or to love the one who was persecuting me. As time has passed God has purged me of that anger and resentment. Love has taken it's place. And with love comes understanding as to WHOM the enemy is. It wasn't my coworker---it was Satan. Love the sinner ---not the sin

90 Days of Prayer
DAY 79

Not every obstacle you face should you question if you're on the right path. Keep going. Prayer, Patience and Purpose. Focus your energy on the people and situations who appreciate and understand you. It will help you to flourish into who you are supposed to be.

"But all too quickly the message is crowded out by the worries of this life, the lure of wealth, and the desire for other things, so no fruit is produced."
- (Mark 4:19)

YOU'RE ON THE RIGHT PATH.

90 Days of Prayer
DAY 80

GOD THE TEACHER,

"For God is working in you, giving you the desire and the power to do what pleases him."
- (Philippians 2:13)

If you have been praying for patience. Know that God is not a magician, He is a teacher. If all of your life you have prayed for patience, and when you look around all you see are people annoying you, pushing your boundaries and testing or trying your patience... that is God, our teacher. He will not just grant you a gift or skill, He will work it out of you. He wants you to know that you have mastered this gift. And He cannot just give it to you, otherwise you won't appreciate nor know how to use it to help others. By Him working it out of you, you can teach another, and they another. Manifesting Him in you, praising Him, not you, and working it out with Him, not through your own means... that's the teacher, that's the God, The Lord Jesus, we serve. He taught the disciples in parables, how else would He teach us?

NOT THE MAGICIAN.

90 Days of Prayer

DAY 81

MAYBE YOU'RE JUST MISUNDERSTOOD. YOU'RE WEIRD, OR

"For My thoughts are not your thoughts,
Nor are your ways My ways," says the Lord.
"For as the heavens are higher than the earth,
So are My ways higher than your ways,
And My thoughts than your thoughts."
- **(Isaiah 55:8-9)**

Loving Jesus openly, or even inwardly--because let's face it, when The Holy Spirit resides in you, you can't do anything without being "different" or "weird" anymore. His ways are not our ways. Being an outsider comes with the territory. Don't be afraid to stand out. Fitting in…Means giving in and settling in. Stand out…Even if you stand alone. Someone will come stand with you. Watch God work. Seek God and His answers will seek you. Live a life you can be EXCITED to tell God about.

Recipe for the week
Falafel Wraps!

Why Eat This?
High fiber, protein, folate, aids in digestion, antioxidants, helps regulate blood sugar, healthy skin, hair and nails. Low glycemic (great for diabetics!) Great for weight-loss, high in vitamin K, mental function and concentration, anti-cancer properties.

Ingredients:

Soaked (not cooked) garbanzo beans (2 cups)

Red onion (1)

Garlic cloves (4)

Parsley (1/4 cup chopped)

Cumin (to taste)

Real Salt (to taste)

Black Pepper (to taste)

Cayenne Pepper (to taste)

How to:

Preheat oven to 415 degrees. Add garbanzo, onion, garlic and parsley to food processor. Pulse until chunky. Add spices. Pulse until batter comes together. (Add 1-2 tbsp water IF necessary! This mixture should be dry, but some water helps it come together.)

Add olive oil to coat bottom of 1-2 pans (depending on how large you make the falafel balls. Roll mixture into 1 inch balls with your hand and place on pan.

Cook for 20-25 min. Rotating them half way through. (If yours are larger they may need more time. If they are smaller they may need more time.)

90 Days of Prayer

DAY 82

THE CROSSROADS

"He is before all things, and in Him all things hold together."
- ***(Colossians 1:17)***

We spend a lot of time, in our cubicles making money, a lot of time in the club making "friends" and a lot of time doing things that we think make us happy." We forget that all of those things are perishable. Nothing in this life is guaranteed. Not your job, your health, loyalty, love, friends or family. But, God, He promised us everlasting love and life, if we follow Him...So why spend your life chasing anything or anyone else but Him? The crossroads. Which side would you choose? That's not to say that you should quit your job, but it is to say, ask God if this is what He intends for you. Are you being a light in the work-place? Are you seeking Christ's heart when it is difficult or not acceptable to do so?

90 Days of Prayer
DAY 83

YOU ARE IRREPLACEABLE!

"For we are his workmanship, created in Christ Jesus for good works, which God prepared beforehand, that we should walk in them." - **(Ephesians 2:10)**

No one can ever replace you...Remember that. Many people may try to replicate, duplicate or imitate the gifts God has given you, but they shall not succeed. Your experiences, your knowledge, your will-power, your laugh, that's unique to just you. Don't ever compare yourself to anyone else. What is meant for you, you will have, and no one can take what God has for YOU..

90 Days of Prayer
DAY 84

SAY WHAT GOD NEEDS YOU TO SAY

"Death and life are in the power of the tongue: and they that love it shall eat the fruit thereof." - **(Proverbs 18:21)**

If you have something good to say, SAY IT. Seems like the only people talking are the ones preaching hate and negativity. Your voice holds weight. Matter of fact life and death is in the power of the tongue. So if you are quiet when God asks you to speak, you could be allowing a death to occur, but if you would just allow God to use you, and speak, you would speak life into someone else and save a life! Don't let the hate and negative comments of the enemy shut you up, because if they do that, they are shutting the God in you up too. Do not let the enemy win the battle for your flesh, allow God to rule over you fully so He may use you for His divine purpose.

90 Days of Prayer
DAY 85

LEAPS!
OF FAITH

Taking a leap of Faith is not walking where we are comfortable, but rather, into a dark, unknown area, where we are no longer in a space where we feel comfortable. Where there is light at the end of the journey, a light that you may or may not see as you start your journey. We must be willing to walk through the valley to get to the light. Be willing to walk. Be willing to wait. Just because it's dark, doesn't mean He isn't there. He is the light, seek the light while you are in the dark places in your life. That may mean taking a leap of faith to get there. Do not be afraid. He goes before you.

"Even though I walk through the valley of the shadow of death, I fear no evil, for You are with me; Your rod and Your staff, they comfort me."

- **(Psalm 23:4)**

90 Days of Prayer
DAY 86

STARTING YOUR DAY WITH JESUS

*"Casting all your anxiety on Him, because He cares for you." - **(1 Peter 5:7)***

I used to start my day with anxiety. Lots of it. How much do I weight today? Is my stomach flat? Did anyone text me last night? Did anyone say good morning? How much money do I have in the bank? Terrible thoughts and dreams and stress none of which belong to me. Talking to God, removes this anxiety. It binds up that anxiety and casts it down to hell where it belongs. I now, wake up and say "Lord, thank you for the night of sleep i just had (be it 2 hours or 9) and Lord, i ask that You anoint my steps today, that I may go and do and see only what You will for me, that I may be a vessel of Your love to everyone I encounter today, in Jesus' Name, Amen." Once you have seen God's love, you can no longer get up and start your day without talking to Him first. Wake up. Be grateful. Pray. Be grateful. Repeat. Be grateful.

90 Days of Prayer
DAY 87

When people say you are "too difficult" it has nothing to do with you. You are forcing them to change to be around you or understand you, being you, is forcing others to have to take a good, hard look at themselves. And when they see their reflection, it is uncomfortable. Just like when we compare ourselves to the Holiness and Sinless life of Jesus Christ.. You have put in the work to set morals and standards that many don't know how to do, or don't want to do. You have CHANGED. Become a new creature in Christ. That's all. Be grateful you have the WILL to stand apart. Don't change. Don't expect many to understand you. Be weird. Be 'difficult,' because that's what the road to redemption looks like-- difficult. But you are brave enough to do it, don't let anyone get in your way, remember, they too, seek to be like Christ, it just may not be in this instant, give them time, just like Christ gave you time.

"Enter through the narrow gate; for the gate is wide and the way is broad that leads to destruction, and there are many who enter through it." -

(Matthew 7:13)

BEING CALLED **WEIRD AND** DIFFICULT.

90 Days of Prayer
DAY 88

"I will give thanks to You, for I am fearfully and wonderfully made; Wonderful are Your works, And my soul knows it very well."

- (Psalm 139:14)

I AM.

This is for anyone who feels less than amazing for being themselves...Repeat to self: I am:, Understanding. Bold in action. Meek. Sensitive. Honest. The 1st first to cry. Emotional. Fearless. Blunt. Moral driven. Transparent. My heart is pure. My intentions are righteous. My heart is with Jesus. My thoughts aren't always the best. I stress out sometimes, and have anxiety other times, but i know Jesus is working on me. I am first on the scene when others are in trouble. I am last to leave at work. I do not steal. I will not cheat. I am loyal and trustworthy. I do not like to gossip, or bash other people. Bullying other people actually hurts me to do. I speak my heart. I am a little weird at times. I smile all of the time. And you know what? These qualities do not make me weak. In fact, they make me strong I am not afraid to be myself! To anyone who feels less than amazing for being themselves...This is who God created me to be, and I'm not perfect. I'm a sinner seeking a merciful God every single day; this is who I am.

90 Days of Prayer
DAY 89

NO EFFORT, NO ENTRY.

"So then we pursue the things which make for peace and the building up of one another."
 - **(Romans 14:9)**

As you journey through life you will make many friends, go on many dates and experience how other people interact with you. Everyone of those people has the opportunity to enter and stay apart in-of your life... If they put in the effort. No effort, no entry. , Is what I go by. Don't sell yourself short. You have worked hard to become that best you can be, why let someone who doesn't see or appreciate that stay? A lot of times those same people, if you allow them to stay without the effort you deserve, will make you feel like less because you will start to judge your worth by their lack of effort. I've learned it's best to love them from a distance as to not hurt myself in the process. God will bring the right people, even if they are but few. And in those people, you will be uplifted, loved and pushed to become a better person in Christ.

Ingredients:

Shredded coconut (no sugar added) (1 cup)

Raw Almond butter (nothing added) (2 tbsp)

Cacao nibs (no sugar added) (1/2 cup)

Coconut Nectar (1/3 cup)

Sesame Tahini (1/4 cup)

Vanilla bean powder (add to desired taste)

Why Eat This?

low glycemic, high omega 3 fats, high fiber, high protein, high antioxidants!

Recipe for the week

Diana's Coconut Cookies!

How to:

Mix all ingredients in a bowl until well combined, scoop out into desired cookie shapes, or even into one large cookie. Bake at 415 degrees for 10-15 minutes (checking every 5, this dessert burns quickly)

Let it cool, and enjoy!

90 Days of Prayer

DAY 90

ACCEPT WHO YOU ARE CALLED TO BE.

> *"Rejoice always, pray without ceasing, in everything give thanks; for this is the will of God in Christ Jesus for you."*
> *- (1 Thessalonians 5:16-18)*

The most dedicated, happy and successful people are not influenced by peer pressure but rather are driven by a fire that burns in them to be not only great but happy being an outcast. Pray for Patience. It takes time to accept who you are called to be. Prayer is the number one way to cast out fear, distractions or feelings of unworthiness that the enemy tries to bring to keep you from who God has called you to be. Pray, and never cease to praise His Name, accepting all things as the goodwill of God for your life. Yes, even the 'bad' things. Although Christ didn't bring the bad upon you, that was the enemy, but in the bad, God can make great things come. Trust Him to do it. When I was diagnosed with my illnesses, I found gratitude in my pain, and for many that concept sounds strange. But praising Him for your misery is giving your misery to Him, obediently, and saying " I trust You Lord, I am afraid and hurt, but I trust You."

Made in the USA
Middletown, DE
20 March 2016